D0475102

ZION
NATIONAL · PARK

Towers of Stone

By J. L. Crawford

Z I O N

Art Direction by:
Sarah Fine

Design/Production by:
Katrina Selzer & Brookie Branch

Edited by:
Carey Vendrame

Copyedited by:
Teresa Roupe

Editorial Assistance by:
Gilda Parodi-Swords

Typesetting by:
The TypeStudio, Santa Barbara CA

SEQUOIA
COMMUNICATIONS

2020 Alameda Padre Serra
Santa Barbara, CA 93103
(805) 963-9336

Copyright 1988 by:
Zion Natural History Association
Zion National Park
Springdale, Utah 84767

(801) 772-3256
This book, or parts thereof, must
not be reproduced in any form
without permission.

Printed in Hong Kong
ISBN: 0-917859-26-X
First Printing, 1988

Cover: The Watchman
Inside front cover: The Virgin River with The
Watchman in the background.
Previous page: Middle Fork of Taylor Creek in
Kolob's Finger Canyons.

PHOTOGRAPHY

J. Cecil Alter: P. 11 inset, 13 top. *Frank Balthis:* P. 5. *Dan Belknap:* Cover, inside front cover - P. 1. *Ralph Clevenger:* P. 7, 22 inset middle & inset right, 24 left, 25 bottom right, 26 right, 29 top left, 29 bottom. *Ed Cooper:* Front flap, P. 25 top left, 34-35. *J.L. Crawford:* P. 6 top, 18, 19 top, 20-21. *Wm. L. Crawford:* P. 8 top. *Joseph Dombrosky:* P. 12 top. *Christine Fancher:* P. 27 top. *Howard Firm (NPS):* P. 12 bottom. *Fred Hirschmann:* P. 14 bottom left, 16 bottom, 19 bottom, 27 bottom, 29 top right, 35 top, 43, back flap. *Frank Jensen:* P. 2-3, 29 middle right, 38-39, 39 bottom right, 40 bottom, 42 left, 44 bottom, back cover. *Dewitt Jones:* P. 22-23, 22 inset left, 23 bottom, 25 top right, 26 left, 47. *John Jones:* P. 6 bottom, 45 bottom. *Mark Kelleher:* Inside back cover, back flap. *Paul Leib:* P. 36 bottom right. *Cara Moore:* P. 9, 24 right, 25 bottom left, 37 top, 46. *Putnam & Valentine:* P. 8 bottom, 10 inset. *Bill Ratcliffe:* P. 16 top, 31 right, 32 top left, center, right, 39 bottom left. *Joseph Romeo:* P. 32-33. *John Telford:* P. 35 bottom, 39 top. *Tom Till:* P. 36 bottom left, 42 right. *Union Pacific:* P. 10-11. *Glenn Van Nimwegen:* P. 14 top, bottom right, 17, 23 top, 28, 29 middle left, 30 left, right, 31 left, 33 top, 36 top, 40 top, 44-45, 45 top. *Dave Wappler:* P. 30 middle, 37 bottom, 38, 41.

Dear Readers:

This publication has been made available by the Zion Natural History Association, a nonprofit corporation working in cooperation with the National Park Service.

This is only one of the many functions we perform that is aimed at increasing the quality of your experience as you visit the many national parks and national monuments. The Association also awards scholarships, and funds interpretive projects, scientific research, publishes free publications, aids in museum and library activities and many other programs for the National Park Service.

The Zion Natural History Association is directed by a voluntary Board of Directors and is supported by the sales of publications, maps and other interpretive items that visitors may purchase at a natural history association sales area. The Association could not continue to assist the National Park Service without your support.

I wish to thank you, the visitor. Through your purchases this is a winning team effort to support the National Park System. Also a special thank you to the Zion Natural History Association Board of Directors for their dedication and guidance.

In this publication we have made available a reorder card for your convenience. This card is also a Zion Natural History Association membership application. If you wish to join, you will enjoy the benefits of membership and stay more informed on our progress and development in the years to come.

Gratefully yours,

Jamie Gentry

Jamie Gentry
Executive Director
Zion Natural
History Association

Author J.L. Crawford was ten years old when the first graded roads were cut through Zion Canyon. He sold farm produce and photographs of the canyon to tourists and tagged along behind the park's first naturalist. Crawford's first book, *Zion Album, A Nostalgic History of Zion,* was published by the Zion Natural History Association in 1986.

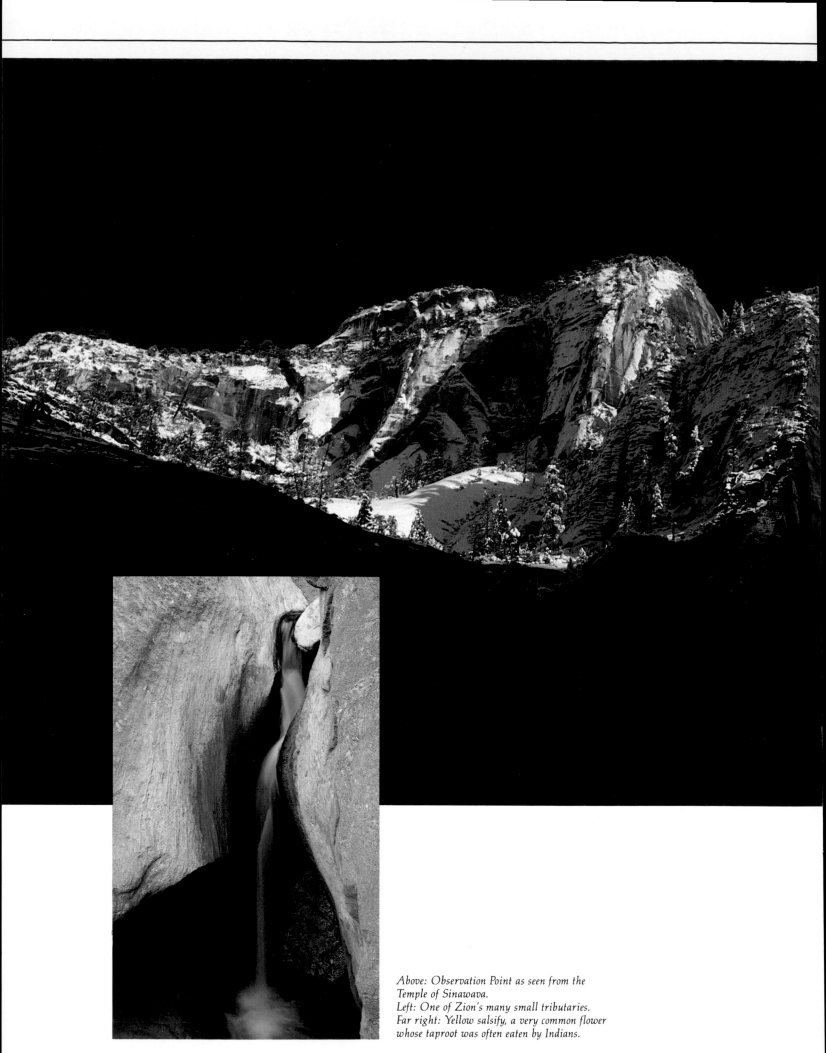

Above: Observation Point as seen from the Temple of Sinawava.
Left: One of Zion's many small tributaries.
Far right: Yellow salsify, a very common flower whose taproot was often eaten by Indians.

CONTENTS

Right: Picnic in the park, early 1920.
Below: Oak Creek Village, circa 1917. Today the area in the bottom, left corner is the site of the Zion Canyon Visitor Center.

Chapter One

EARLY INHABITANTS

The first known residents of Zion were the Basket Makers. They were seminomadic Indians who eventually evolved into the Pueblo culture as their lifestyle became more sedentary and their means of subsistence changed from primarily hunting to growing and storing crops. The Pueblos, now known as Anasazi (Navajo for "Ancient Ones"), occupied Zion from 500 A.D. to about 1200 A.D. This culture began to decline earlier in the Zion area than it did in the center of the Anasazi region (an area called "Four Corners," where the borders of Utah, Arizona, New Mexico and Colorado meet), probably due to pressure from enemies to the north and west. Consequently, the elaborate pueblos common to the Four Corners area are not found here. Pictographs and petroglyphs have been found, along with a few food storage bins constructed of mud and stone. Archeologists have unearthed the foundation of what appears to have been an extensive building that was constructed of mud and rocks—a multiroomed masonry pueblo that housed several families. Artifacts indicate that the occupants grew corn, squash, and beans and hunted turkeys, deer, and bighorn sheep.

Following the Anasazi, several Paiute Indian subtribes occupied the region. They were of Shoshonean stock and were subject to the greater Ute tribe to the north, whose chief exacted annual tributes from the weaker tribes. Children were often taken as an offering when other commodities were lacking. This practice became more prevalent during the Spanish era, as the slave trade proved to be quite lucrative. Domination by the Utes, and frequent raids by Navajos from across the Colorado River had rendered the local Paiutes destitute by the time the Mormons took possession of the area.

A small subtribe called the Parusits occupied the stretch of the Virgin River (they called it Pah-roos) below Zion Canyon. They had no permanent dwellings, but moved up and down the river and into adjacent areas on a seasonal basis, entering the canyon only to gather food and hunt game. They regarded the canyon with fear and respect as it was the home of two of their deities.

The Parrusits did some primitive farming along the river, but their meager diet consisted mostly of wild seeds, roots, lizards, and insects. No doubt their lot improved with the advent of the Mormon settlers, although some of the tribes lost their identity entirely. Those who remained adopted the ways of those who displaced them, and now live in towns and on reservations.

The first recorded visit to southwestern Utah by Europeans was made in 1776 by the Dominguez-Escalante expedition on their return from abandoning a quest to find a northern route to California. On the verge of starvation, they followed the Hurricane Fault scarp southward and passed within 20 miles of Zion Canyon. They noted the high mesas to the east but did no exploring.

Fifty years later, Jedediah Smith, with a party of 16 men, passed by in the tracks of the Spaniards. They were fur traders in search of beaver pelts but were more intent on finding a route to California, so they failed to find the canyon.

Several military and geographic explorations were carried out in the surrounding area before the arrival of the Mormons, but Zion remained unknown to them until 1858 when Nephi Johnson, a young missionary to the Indians, and interpreter for immigrant parties passing through the area, explored the upper Virgin River on Brigham Young's orders. The Mormons sought out areas rich in natural resources to build self-sufficient communities and expand their economic, cultural, and ecclesiastical interests.

Several communities, including Springdale, were soon established along the river, at the mouth of Zion Canyon. Isaac Behunin, one of the Springdale settlers, built a cabin near the present site of the Zion Lodge where he farmed for several years. It was Behunin who thought of the name "Zion" for the canyon.

Zion became known through the work of artists, photographers, and writers in the late 1800s and early 1900s. But the publicity Zion received had little effect on travel to the area because the roads were little more than trails.

In 1908 a U.S. government deputy surveyor named Leo Snow was hired

to survey the township that includes Zion Canyon. He was so impressed with the scenery that in his report the following year he recommended that the canyon be made a national park. On July 31, 1909, a month after the letter reached the office of the secretary of the interior, President Taft signed a proclamation creating Mukuntuweap National Monument. Ten years later the name was changed to Zion National Monument.

The designation of the canyon as a national monument opened the way for making the region accessible, but changes were slow in coming. While the approach road to the canyon was still primarily on the flood plain of the river, the residents of Springdale and Zion were exploring the possibility of a road through Pine Creek that would shorten the distance to ranches, to timber areas, and to markets where they sold their farm produce.

One of the principal advocates of such a route was John Winder, who owned a ranch on the East Rim of Zion. A second generation pioneer, Winder was a colorful character in Zion's history. He was an orphan without formal education, who was described by a contemporary as "tough as boiled owl and weighed less than a sack of beans soaking wet."

Background photo: Utah Park's company buses at the Temple of Sinawava.
Inset left: William Wylie operated this tourist camp in Zion Canyon from 1917-1923.
Inset right: Second-generation pioneer John Winder in Echo Canyon.

About the turn of the century, Winder and his neighbors built a trail up the east wall to his ranch over which livestock could be driven. The trail is still maintained by the National Park Service as the East Rim Trail. But Winder had a shorter route that he used when he was in a hurry to get to or from the ranch. It wasn't a trail, but rather a shortcut through the narrow gorge of Pine Creek that necessitated some cliff scaling. This is the route over which he guided the engineers who surveyed the Zion Tunnel. The completion of the tunnel in 1930 brought Winder's greatest dream to fruition.

Zion received a $15,000 appropriation for road improvements in 1916. At the same time, convicts from the Utah State Penetentiary were building an approach road along the foothills, which eliminated the many fords in the river.

In 1917 the Wylie Way Camp was established, and was replaced by the modern Zion Lodge in 1925. Zion became a national park in 1919. This new status brought about other improvements, including the completion of the Zion-Mt. Carmel Highway in 1930. The highway shortened the distance to Bryce Canyon by 70 miles, and to the Grand Canyon by 20 miles. Best of all, it eliminated a hazardous stretch of mountain road through the Arizona Strip.

The Civilian Conservation Corps in Zion

Fulfilling his campaign promise to put a million boys to work planting trees in the national forests, Franklin D. Roosevelt launched the Civilian Conservation Corps in 1933. Though the original plan was to place 200,000 young men in 1,000 camps, by April 1933 there were 300,000 men in nearly 1,500 camps.

Horace M. Albright, who was the director of the National Park Service, served on the organizing committee and had the specific job of placing the camps and outlining the work to be done. Consequently, the national parks were primary beneficiaries of this program. Camps were started in national parks, national forests, and state parks. These federal and state agencies had the responsibility of carrying out the work projects, while the U.S. Army operated the camps. Zion was the site of two CCC camps.

The Depression caused such severe cuts in funds to the national parks that the work of the CCC was particularly important. At Zion, the CCC constructed several buildings out of dressed stone, as well as entrance stations and sign posts. Much of the park's boundary was fenced, riverbank stabilization was a major project, and rock curbing was installed at most parking areas. One or two new trails were built and road maintenance was an ongoing project. A few workers felt privileged to assist with archeological digs and bird and animal studies.

Zion had an educational advisor for the two camps and night classes were popular and well attended. Park rangers, project foremen, and even some enrollees served as instructors. Many young men found their careers as a result of their work or the training they received in the CCC.

World War II brought an end to the CCC, but what Zion gained from that Depression-born organization will be long lasting.

Left: Stone sign posts such as this one were constructed by the CCC.
Below: The Bridge Mountain CCC camp (1935) was the first of two camps that were established in Zion.

The Cable Story

Inconspicuously located at the beginning of the East Rim Trail at the base of Cable Mountain, is a small rock monument on which is mounted a metal plaque explaining the wooden structure perched precariously 2,000 feet above. It is all that is left of a device that for a quarter of a century brought lumber off the mountain, and its story is a fascinating part of Zion's history.

Dave Flanigan, a young resident of Springdale, had seen a contraption consisting of wire and pulleys carry the mail up and down a mountain near Shunesburg. He thought that a similar but heavier machine could be built to carry lumber off the plateau into the valley below. Several years later, with the help of his brother William, Dave completed the prototype. Only gravity was used for power; the force of a loaded basket coming down would propel an empty one up from the bottom.

The Flanigan brothers were plagued by setbacks during and after construction. Heavy loads caused runaways and overheating of the pulleys, so a braking system had to be devised.

The cable began operation on August 1, 1901, but it was four more years before Dave, William, and two other Flanigan brothers purchased a

sawmill to produce lumber to transport over it. The work of logging, repairing breakdowns, contending with bad roads, and marketing problems had everyone discouraged.

In 1907 Dave sold the mill and the cable. The system changed hands twice more, and was never profitable for any of the owners, but it did fill a need for the Virgin River communities until better roads and transportation were available.

Left: In addition to the Zion Cable, David Flanigan invented a constant velocity universal joint, a helicopter, and a windmill. Above: The unloading platform of the Zion Cable (1913).

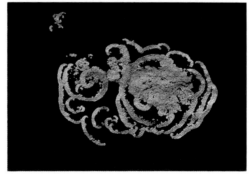

Top: Wind and water have created fluted
sandstone walls such as this throughout the park.
Above: Lichens add interesting shapes, and after
rainfalls, vivid color, to rock surfaces.
Left: Patterns such as this are often created by
exfoliation, a process resulting from the expansion
of a rock surface, causing thin slabs of rock to
break loose.

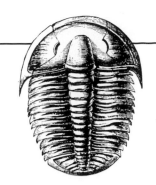

Chapter Two

GEOLOGICAL HISTORY

Zion is nature's geologic masterpiece. Powerful forces of wind, water, and volcanic fire over millions of years shaped the earth into a landscape of unsurpassed beauty and grandeur.

The history of Zion is told in its rocks. It began 240 million years ago, before the appearance of the first dinosaurs. The rocks of Zion were formed one layer above the other, in orderly succession. Geologists call these layers of sedimentary rocks "formations." They differ from each other in features such as thickness and mineral and fossil content. Each formation reveals the secrets of its time: the geography, climate, and the plants and animals that lived then. At Zion there are seven formations, each made up of different materials and each telling a different story. These formations, from oldest to youngest, are the Moenkopi, the Chinle, the Moenave, the Kayenta, the Navajo Sandstone, the Temple Cap, and the Carmel. The oldest formation appears at the bottoms of the deepest canyons, while the youngest appears at the tops of some of Zion's tallest features.

The most important formation at Zion Canyon is Navajo Sandstone. It is essentially a huge mass of homogeneous, fine-grained sandstone. Zion owes its grandeur to this massive rock layer that forms the canyon's 2,000-foot-high vertical walls. This formation covers a total area of approximately 150,000 square miles extending from central Wyoming to southwestern California. Wherever Navajo Sandstone is exposed, streams have carved canyons into it, some of which far exceed Zion Canyon in length. Yet Zion is unique. Here the Navajo Sandstone reaches its maximum thickness of nearly 2,400 feet at the Temple of Sinawava. Valleys and side canyons have notched the skyline into many monoliths, and given each a distinct personality.

An interesting characteristic of the Navajo Formation is exemplified in the Zion Narrows, where the North Fork of the Virgin River has cut through the rock for hundreds of feet without widening the gorge. This holds true until the channel reaches the softer layers below the Navajo. This has happened at the Temple of Sinawava, where the river emerges from the Narrows. Here the river bed is in the Kayenta layer and the canyon begins to widen perceptibly. The softer layers of rock allow undercutting of the cliffs which, being weakened by the thousands of vertical fractures and joints, split off, usually in long

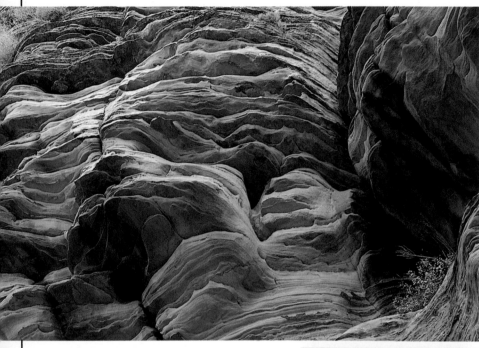

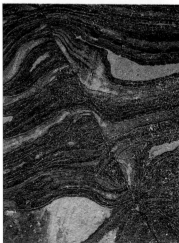

Above & right: Erosion and time have created a myriad of shapes and patterns in the sandstone.
Opposite: Yellow cliff columbine in one of Zion's many hanging gardens.

columns, leaving smooth walls above. This is the process that keeps the walls of Zion Canyon vertical.

Another unique feature of Navajo Sandstone is its exceptionally porous nature. This porosity allows water from rain and melting snow to accumulate, and as the droplets migrate downward, the rock becomes saturated. When the water reaches the more compact and impervious layer of stone contained in the Kayenta Formation, its downward path is blocked. The water then moves horizontally to the surface and emerges in the form of springs and seeps, creating Zion's famous "spring line." This phenomenon gives life to hanging gardens and creates arches and overhangs by dissolving the lime that cements the sand grains together, thus undermining and weakening the heavy rock burden above.

The spectacular, sculptured Navajo Sandstone is what Zion is famous for, but the other six formations have also played a part in shaping Zion and add much to its color and charm. The Moenkopi Formation (the bottom layer) is displayed as a series of brightly colored bands, indicating both marine and stream deposits. The Chinle Formation consists of a solid cliff of coarse sand and gravel (Shinarump Conglomerate). Above

The Sentinel Landslide (above) was one of many Zion-area landslides, which have left the "slump" hills that surround Springdale. Slump hills are the result of large volumes of rock or loose debris moving en masse down a slope.

this are deposits of softer material in colors of gray, purple, and white that contain uranium, fossilized bones, and petrified wood. The Moenave Formation is made up of layers of shales below and sandstones above in colors of pink, purple, and red. The presence of fish scales and skeletal parts in the bottom layers indicates an evolvement from lakes and sluggish streams to a more terrestrial environment and swifter streams. The Kayenta Formation is made up of red and mauve siltstones and sandstones, indicating deposition by low to moderate energy streams on a broad flood plain, where dinosaurs left their tracks. The Temple Cap Formation is a thin layer of heavily pigmented clay, silt, and sandstone, the source of the red streaking that stains the upper faces of Navajo Sandstone. The Carmel Formation is both the youngest, and the uppermost of the formations that are exposed within the park. It is the least significant formation from a viewer's standpoint, but important in that it is composed primarily of fossil-bearing marine limestone, which proves that the ocean moved in over the desert

sands and provided the calcareous cementing material in the Navajo Sandstone. Also, the varying thicknesses of the formation (from a few feet to 240 feet) and the presence of volcanic fragments indicate the beginning of crustal movements and volcanic activity.

The seven layers of rock at Zion tell of the many changes endured by the park. It has been covered by an ocean and swept by desert winds. It has experienced earthquakes, volcanic eruptions, and rockfalls of gigantic proportions.

But by far the most important factor in the present formation of Zion Canyon is the Virgin River— the seemingly placid stream that still flows through it. Over a period of hundreds of thousands of years, water from the Virgin River and tributary streams has moved swiftly over a rock that disintegrates easily, resulting in the carving of enormous gorges.

The forces of nature are still at work in Zion. From a geological standpoint it is young. It will undoubtedly look very different one million years from now, so enjoy the view while you can!

The Petrified Forest

The Petrified Forest consists of ancient trees and remains of other formerly living things, that gradually turned to stone in a geological process taking millions of years. Zion's Petrified Forest is located in the southwest corner of the park and is actually an extension of the better known Petrified Forest National Park in Arizona. The petrified wood found here, however, is opaque and dull colored and not of gem quality. The hard bottom layer of the Chinle Formation consists partially of broken logs, and small petrified wood fragments are found throughout the upper soft shales of the multicolored, or "painted desert" layers.

Petrified logs in the Shinarump Conglomerate of the Chinle Formation.

Just Imagine

Dinosaur tracks in the Kayenta shale of the Left Fork of North Creek, Kolob Canyons.

It isn't hard to believe that dinosaurs existed when you look at a skeleton of one in a museum; and it is easy to visualize what one must have looked like when you see several tracks in the Kayenta shale of the Left Fork of North Creek. But it is difficult to realize that the tracks are 170,000,000 years old, and that instead of a narrow canyon, Zion was a vast tropical flood plain.

A visit to Zion as recently as a million years ago would have resulted in a completely different experience than a visit today. Imagine going into the Narrows a ways and not seeing the Great White Throne. Then, upon leaving the canyon you just miss getting caught by the Horse Valley landslide.

Next imagine a visit to Zion a few million years from now. The Watchman and Johnson Mountain are low red buttes. There are a few pinnacles similar to Eagle Crags where the West Temple used to be. The Great White Throne has become a conical point resembling the North Guardian Angel. A massive landslide near the Mountain of Mystery has created a lake, inundating campgrounds and roads. The Virgin River has worked its way into the Markagunt Plateau, creating a new Zion Narrows beyond Old State Route 14 and robbing the Sevier River of half its water. Paiute and Sevier Bridge reservoirs are gone and farms throughout central Utah have been replaced by sagebrush desert.

We will never see the day, but just imagine!

MT. KINESAVA

TEMPLE CAP FORMATION

NAVAJO FORMATION

KAYENTA FORMATION

MOENAVE FORMATION

CHINLE FORMATION

PETRIFIED FOREST

TOWN OF ROCKVILLE

WEST TEMPLE

ZION CANYON

THE SENTINEL

SPRINGDALE SANDSTONE (MEMBER OF MOENAVE)

SHINARUMP CONGLOMERATE (MEMBER OF CHINLE)

MOENKOPI FORMATION

Six of Zion's layers of sedimentary rock, which are referred to as "formations," can be seen in this panoramic photograph taken near Smithsonian Butte. Each telling a different story, the formations are pointed out here beginning with the Temple Cap and ending with the Moenkopi. The Carmel Formation, Zion's youngest, is not visible here. The Springdale Sandstone and the Shinarump Conglomerate are parts of the Moenave and Chinle

Chapter Three

FLORA AND FAUNA

Zion is home to a wide variety of plant and animal life. Shaded canyons and open, sunny slopes create environmental extremes from moist forests to rugged deserts. Plants and animals suited to these diverse conditions have evolved over time and live side by side in a delicate ecological balance.

MAMMALS

Nearly everyone who visits the park sees some of Zion's 68 kinds of mammals, 36 kinds of reptiles, 7 kinds of amphibians, and 271 species of birds.

The mule deer resides throughout the area and is the largest mammal one is likely to see in the park. A few elk reside in the higher Kolob Plateau to the north, but generally they prefer more open country than the park provides. Desert bighorn sheep were native to the area but disappeared prior to 1950. Though they have been reintroduced, they're seldom seen.

Predators include the mountain lion (also commonly called cougar), bobcat, coyote, gray fox, badger, and the weasel. The one known shrew is classed as an insectivore, along with several species of bats. Bears, wolves, and otters have long since disappeared from Zion. Raccoons were once numerous, but

disappeared during the 1920s. Should you be driving through the canyon at night, you might spot a relative of the raccoon—the ringtail cat. This handsome creature is nocturnal and may raid your camp looking for food.

Of the many rodents in the park, the most obvious is the gray rock squirrel, which is sometimes a nuisance to campers. Less numerous, but more likely to be seen at any time of year, is the little antelope ground squirrel. The pocket gopher may never be seen, but his mounds are numerous at all elevations. Likewise, the presence of the wood rat, or pack rat, is evidenced by the many "trash piles" this nighttime raider builds around the entrances to his dens.

Porcupines are still present, but are more numerous on the plateau

Previous page: A brilliantly colored stand of aspen in Kolob Canyons.
Inset photos: The badger is one of Zion's common predators (left). The notoriously bold Stellar's jay resides primarily in coniferous forests (middle). The whitetail prairie dog is a diurnal burrower that feeds on plants (right).
Above: Short-horned lizards are active during daytime hours and feed on ants and other insects.
Top right: Though ferocious looking, tarantulas are relatively harmless.

than in the canyon. Beavers were absent from the park for 50 years, but reappeared in about 1940 while migrating up the Virgin River from the Colorado. They are called "bank beavers" since they live in burrows and generally don't build dams. Cottontails and jackrabbits are found in the park, but jackrabbits seldom venture into the canyon.

REPTILES AND AMPHIBIANS

Nonvenomous reptiles and amphibians make up an interesting part of Zion's fauna. The most visible among these are lizards, the largest being the vegetarian chuckwalla, which may reach a length of 20 inches. The most colorful lizards are the hardest to see because they are rare and well camouflaged. These are the collared lizard, the banded gecko, and the western skink. The whiptails are also colorful and numerous. They have long, slender, striped bodies and the tails of the young range in color from blue to green. The two species of horned lizards are the desert horned lizard, which is nearly always seen below 5,500 feet and the short-horned lizard, which stays above 6,000 feet.

Like the horned lizards, some of Zion's snakes are particular about their habitat range. For example, the black and white banded common kingsnake is seldom, if ever, found above 4,500 feet and its more colorful cousin, the Sonoran Mountain kingsnake, has never been seen below 6,500 feet. This species is quite rare and is often persecuted because of its resemblance to the venomous coral snake. Should you come upon a snake that is banded in red, white, and black (or perhaps pink, cream, and black), remember that the white (or cream) and red (or pink) are separated by black in the harmless species. Also remember that there are no coral snakes in Zion.

The western rattler is a venomous snake that may be found at all elevations up to 8,000 feet. Though it may appear threatening if startled or cornered, it will always seek an escape route. The venom is not as virulent as that of some other species, but it can be deadly, nevertheless.

BIRDS

About 271 species of birds have been recorded in Zion. Of this number, about 60 are permanent residents and over 100 are known to breed in the area, including three kinds of hummingbirds, the golden eagle, and the rare peregrine falcon. The singing birds include robins, black headed grosbeaks, solitary and warbling vireos, lazuli buntings and, in October, Townsend's solitaires.

Clockwise from top left: This hornet's nest appears to be growing out of the rock. ◆ A moth resting on similarly colored rocks. ◆ The common raven is a carrion feeder that is found throughout the park. ◆ The mule deer is the largest mammal one is likely to see in the park.

The canyon wren's song—a clear, sweet cascade of descending notes—can be heard any month of the year. The most unlikely song is that of the water ouzel, or dipper. The ungainly, soot-colored ouzel has a surprisingly pretty song, but since it dives into swift streams for food, it is hard to hear since it always sings to the accompaniment of a babbling brook or waterfall. A hanging garden is a favorite nesting place, with the nest being hidden underneath a projection of dripping tufa and vegetation. Other choice nesting sites are behind waterfalls and in damp caves.

Seven members of the crow family are known to Zion, three of which nest there. The raven and scrub jay are ever present and the Steller's jay frequents the canyon from his normal range in the higher elevations. With the exception of the rare gray jay, these are the noisiest birds in the park. The call of the gregarious pinyon jay always precedes his arrival. This species is called the "blue crow," but it is less objectionable than the black crow. Great flocks of them appear throughout the pinyon-juniper belt. Ravens are notorious clowns and bullies and take delight in making life miserable for the soaring hawks and eagles, whom they dive bomb repeatedly. The ravens usually win these encounters.

Also considered a clown by some is the roadrunner, a member of the cuckoo family. His method of locomotion and obtaining meals may appear comical, but he is dead serious when he flails a rattlesnake to death and swallows it whole. The roadrunner is a desert dweller, but has been observed among the aspen trees in late summer, at an elevation of 9,000 feet.

ANIMALS AND YOUR SAFETY

No wild animal is a threat to humans as long as it is treated as a wild creature and not as a pet. Even a tame-appearing deer could inflict a wound with a hoof or antler. One potentially harmful animal that hikers often ask about is the mountain lion. No attack on a human by one of these retiring animals has been reported. Fortunate indeed is the visitor who catches sight of one, as most residents of the area never do, although their tracks are ever present, especially in the Kolob district. As with the rattlesnake, if you should meet a cougar, give him an opportunity to leave. More than likely, one will see you but you will never see it.

Just a word of warning in case you should find a fox that appears tame or sick, or a bat that appears lost, DON'T TOUCH! These animals are known to carry rabies and should be reported to the rangers.

The tarantula is a large hairy spider that comes out of hiding in late summer and fall to look for a mate. This species has been severely persecuted as it was thought to be deadly. But the fact is that it is entirely harmless. Its bite may be painful, but not life-threatening. Let them live, as they consume a lot of insects.

Don't kill any snakes. If a rattler is near your camp call a ranger to remove it. Learn to distinguish between rattlesnakes and gopher snakes. Gopher snakes are the largest of Zion's reptiles, and may attain a length of six feet. They are gentle and can be handled, but it isn't recommended.

*Left: Mule deer.
Right: The innocent-looking rock squirrel is sometimes a nuisance to campers.*

Z I O N

The Virgin River

Zion Canyon was carved and shaped by the Virgin River, a tributary of the Colorado River, which is nine times as long and 50 times larger by volume, but has only one seventh the gradient factor. Two main branches make up the Virgin River: the North Fork (Mukuntuweap), which originates as springs north of Zion's north boundary at an elevation of 9,000 feet, and the East Fork (Parunuweap), which originates in similar highlands east of the North Fork and drains Long Valley, which runs along Highway 89. The Virgin River is about 160 miles long and empties into Lake Mead, some 25 miles from the Colorado River. There is a total drop of 7,800 feet, for an average of 48 feet per mile. This gradient increases to 76 feet per mile through Zion Canyon.

Where the North Fork passes the park headquarters, the average flow is 100 cubic feet per second; however it has been known to slow to 20 cubic feet per second following several dry years. Although the stream may appear quite clear much of the time, it is always carrying fine suspended silt. Enough in fact, to fill 30 dump trucks (120 cubic yards) in a 24-hour period. It is estimated that a flood of 10 times the normal flow can carry 2,000 times as much solid material. One hour of flooding can remove more silt, sand, and gravel than one year of normal flow. In addition to the usual month or more of run off from snowmelt in the spring, floods may occur many times a year. This makes it easy to understand how the little Virgin River could carry cubic miles of earth over the eons.

PLANTS AND WILDFLOWERS

A great variety of plants thrive in Zion. Shady side canyons, rapid changes in elevation, and disparate sources of water provide diverse environments for biotic communities. Consequently, plants requiring very little water cover desert hills and live only a short distance from the lush greenery that grows along the banks of the Virgin River.

·The most noticeable plant community below 5,000 feet is the pinyon-juniper association, known throughout the west as the "pygmy forest." It dominates the talus slopes and sandy benches below the vertical cliffs of Zion. Scattered among those evergreen species are serviceberry, singleleaf ash, roundleaf buffaloberry, manzanita, joint fir, cliffrose and cacti. Gambel oak, scrub live oak and bigtooth maple also appear in patches.

Second to the pygmy forest in the canyon is the riparian woodland, a narrow band of deciduous trees along the river and its tributaries. The Fremont cottonwood is dominant, and is the largest of the riverbank varieties, followed by the box elder and velvet ash. Several kinds of willows are also common. Water birch occurs primarily in the very wet areas in side canyons. The ground cover in this community has undergone considerable change since the occupation of the canyon. Where sandbar willows and wild roses used to dominate, the exotic tamarisk, or salt cedar, has largely taken over and forms dense thickets in many places.

The terraces and plateaus from 5,500 to 7,500 feet are characterized by ponderosa pine (largest of local conifers), Rocky Mountain juniper, and sagebrush. Gambel oak is also prominent at this elevation, sometimes attaining the size of a small tree. Douglas fir and white fir are also fairly abundant, although they usually live, along with the quaking aspens, at higher elevations. The 14 varieties of cacti that have

Opposite: Zion's side canyons are replete with moss-lined waterfalls such as this one.
Clockwise from left: Showy goldeneye; greenleaf manzanita; claret cup cactus; hoary aster; shooting star.

Left: A lone yucca stands alongside a weathered and dying ponderosa pine. Above: Detail of a prickly-pear cactus. Right: Beavertail cactus.

been identified in Zion, are divided into three groups commonly called: hedgehog, cholla (commonly referred to as tree cactus), and prickly pear. Identification, especially among the prickly pears and chollas, is difficult and confusing because they hybridize so readily. The most colorful, if not the most abundant, of Zion's wildflowers are found in the cactus family. The claret cup, smallest of the hedgehogs, is the first to bloom, sometimes beginning in early March, followed by its larger cousin, the purple torch. Some varieties may bloom as late as August, but the best shows are in May and June.

Two kinds of yuccas grow in Zion. One, the narrowleaf or Spanish bayonet, produces a flower stalk of white blossoms reaching several feet above the spines, inspiring the popular name, The Lord's candle-stick. The yuccas, which belong to

the lily family, are erroneously called cacti by some and, along with the cacti, are considered "desert" plants. Zion is a desert canyon, and has an average annual rainfall of about 15 inches, so both cacti and yuccas are perfectly at home throughout the park, even up to 7,500 feet in areas with southern exposure.

If the desert plants seem out of place on the plateau tops, likewise, several mountain varieties are found at the bottom of the canyon in areas of limited sunlight and adequate moisture. In Emerald Pools Canyon, for instance, entirely different plant communities face each other from opposite sides of the canyon, though they are only a few hundred feet apart. At the end of the Gateway to the Narrows Trail, a yucca grows on a cliff ledge just a few yards directly above a Douglas fir tree. Hanging gardens exist at several places where

water seeps constantly from the vertical rock walls, depositing calcareous tufa, which gives footing and life to a variety of water-loving plants. The two most accessible hanging gardens are at Weeping Rock and along the Gateway to the Narrows Trail. In addition to grasses and banks of maidenhair ferns, such flowers as cliff columbine, shooting star, purple violet and scarlet monkey flower grow abundantly. The latter species blooms in spring and again in September. Scarlet lobelia, or cardinal flower, while not a part of the "vertical" garden, may be found nearby in late summer.

Left: Ponderosa pines silhouetted against the evening sky.
Above: Needle clusters from a ponderosa pine.

From the east end of the Zion tunnel to the East Entrance to the park, the Zion-Mt. Carmel Highway winds about eight miles through cuts and around contours in the upper half of the massive Navajo Sandstone, an area known as "slickrock." On these sandstone slopes ponderosa pine, littleleaf mountain mahogany, as well as Douglas fir and Rocky Mountain juniper appear to be growing out of solid rock. As this side canyon widens into a sandy valley bottom near the East Entrance, ponderosa and juniper are joined by Gambel oak, sagebrush, manzanita, and joint

fir. Manzanita and joint fir are also found, though in fewer numbers, on the rocky slopes and sandy benches of the main canyon.

It seems odd that the first blossoms of spring may appear here instead of in the lower elevations. The tiny pink Japanese-lantern blossoms of the manzanita usually begin to appear in January, and have been known to bloom in December, at an elevation of 6,000 feet. The low-growing sand buttercup blooms in March, or earlier, in the sandy areas near the east end of the tunnel. Small, brilliant, orange-scarlet clumps of slickrock paintbrush dot

the slopes. Look for purplish-blue spiderwort along the roadsides and other sandy areas. Red and purple penstemons bloom along the road sides throughout the summer, but the latest flower to bloom in this section of the park is the bright red hummingbird trumpet, which looks like penstemon but belongs to the evening primrose family.

Perhaps the best color display of all is the bigtooth maple, which turns brilliant shades of red before dropping its leaves in October. It grows along the streambed of Clear Creek, the drainage that the road follows through the slickrock area.

A few species catch everyone's eyes, depending on the time of year. For a short period in early spring, the disturbed areas on the canyon floor become solid purple from the bloom of the foul-smelling member of the mustard family, *Chorispora tenella*.

It seems to have been introduced within the last two decades and has no common name. Desert beauty, also known as "purple sage," is an early blooming shrub belonging to the pea family. The real purple sage blossoms a little later and is very conspicuous on the hills near the Zion Canyon Visitor Center for only a few days. The tall yellow spikes of another mustard, the princesplume, has wide distribution on the rocky slopes and some blossoms remain throughout the summer. Perhaps the biggest attention-getter in the park is the sacred datura, a member of the nightshade family, which may have as many as a hundred large, white, funnel-shaped flowers on one plant. The blossoms open at night and remain open most of the day. This is the lowly jimson (or Jamestown) weed, but it has become so abundant here that it now has the nickname "Zion lily."

A small tree that is not widely distributed and could go unnoticed except when it's in bloom, is the New Mexico locust (*Robinia neomexicana*). When it blooms, the aroma is delightful. Best seen along the road near Weeping Rock and near the west door of the Zion Canyon Visitor Center, the New Mexico locust's clusters of pink flowers bloom a second time if summer showers are abundant.

Top (L-R): Riverbank grass; manzanita; maidenhair fern; sacred datura, or "Zion lily." Bottom: A pinyon pine appears to be growing out of solid rock.

Chapter Four

LANDMARKS

Zion's dramatic landscape is filled with many remarkable geologic features. Its jutting rocks, high plateaus, broad mesas, towering cliffs, and deep canyons form breathtaking scenic vistas that have thrilled visitors for hundreds of years. Certain features are so extraordinary that they are considered landmarks. Long before the establishment of Zion as a national park, these natural creations marked the way for pioneers and visitors. Names such as the Great White Throne, the Temple of Sinawava, and the Towers of the Virgin reflect the exalted emotions people felt when they looked upon these monumental works of nature highlights in a landscape where the spectacular is commonplace.

GATEWAY TO THE NARROWS

The Gateway to the Narrows is probably the easiest and most popular of Zion's nature trails. The paved section of the trail begins where the scenic drive ends at the Temple of Sinawava. It parallels the river for one mile, and ends at the point where the canyon narrows significantly, requiring hikers to take to the water.

A canopied interpretive facility is located at the trailhead, and interpretive signs are placed along the way. A hard-surfaced trail with very little incline, The Gateway to

the Narrows is suitable for wheelchairs (with assistance) and strollers. Naturalist-guided walks are scheduled to point out the many interesting features along the way. Among the highlights is a desert swamp that contains typical water-growing plants, leopard frogs, and a spring with a constant temperature of 70 degrees Fahrenheit, plus or minus one degree. You will also see The Stadium with its arched canyon walls, and may hear the billy-goat call of the canyon tree frog. The most luxuriant of Zion's hanging gardens is here; and living among the many flowering plants is the Zion snail, found nowhere else in the world. Dark brown to black in color, full-size snails are only about one-eighth inch in diameter. Birds become less noticeable as the canyon narrows, but look for the dipper (water ouzel), black phoebe, canyon wren, and the winter wren.

The view of the Mountain of Mystery at the end of the trail is spectacular, but if the river is higher than usual, the sight may require getting your feet wet.

WEST TEMPLE & TOWERS OF THE VIRGIN

While the Great White Throne has become, to many, the symbol of Zion, the West Temple is the beacon. Early travelers used it as a guide and it is viewed by thousands annually who never get to the park because it can be seen from afar in several directions. The West Temple dominates the landscape with its position, height, and distinctive symmetry, which set it apart from its otherwise homogeneous companions, the Towers of the Virgin.

In 1903 it was described by Frederick S. Dellenbaugh as "a . . .Titanic mountain of bare rock, the Great Temple of the Virgin, lifting its opalescent shoulders alluringly against the eastern sky."

The temple is located near the southwest corner of park, and is the highest point on the canyon wall. As viewed from The Zion Canyon Visitor Center, the West Temple and Altar of Sacrifice, with several pinnacles in between, form the headwall of Oak Creek Canyon, which has been called the greatest skyline in the world.

The East Temple, on the opposite side of the canyon, is less imposing, being about 700 feet lower. It, too, is crowned by the red Temple Cap Formation, which gives the East and West Temples a terraced or "decked" appearance.

The Temple Cap appears on several other peaks, and while it isn't visible on the Altar of Sacrifice, a remnant of it provides the red wash from which this feature gets its name.

Moonsets, lightning storms, stream channels cutting through rock faces, and frozen waterfalls create a variety of moods.

KOLOB CANYONS

The Kolob Canyons section of the park, located in Zion's northwest corner, has an appeal and grandeur all its own. Kolob's Finger Canyons are as dramatic and awe-inspiring as any sight in Zion. To get to them, take Exit 40 from Interstate 15, about 18 miles south of Cedar City and 27 miles north of St. George.

A 5.2-mile-long spur road leads up Taylor Creek, over Lee Pass, and into the Timber Creek drainage. It is here that one sees an entirely different Zion. Looming to the left are the fingers of Navajo Sandstone, with narrow canyons, 1,600 feet deep, in between. In Kolob Canyons the Navajo Formation is red, or salmon-colored all the way to the top.

The sharp eastward dip of the strata reveals secrets of Zion's past. Two geologic events, about one hundred million years apart, were largely responsible for shaping this part of the park. First there was compression of the earth's crust, causing a north-south wrinkle, or anticline, which has been named the Kanarra Fold. The second event resulted in the Hurricane Fault. A crack in the earth split Kanarra Fold along its axis, pushing the east side upward much higher than the west. Subsequent erosion has resulted in further exposure of this fault.

One of Kolob Canyons' most impressive sights is the magnificent Kolob Arch, whose 310-foot span makes it possibly the largest freestanding arch in the world. Visitors who take the seven-mile hike to Kolob Arch are treated to a spectacular view of the arch from the canyon floor.

SLICKROCK

The "slickrock" area of Zion has no definite boundaries and the name is unofficial, but it is generally considered to be the area between the tunnel and the East Entrance to the park. This eight-mile section of the park must resemble, except for the green trees and shrubs, the vast desert of sand dunes that it was 140 million years ago.

The term slickrock was probably coined by a local rancher who watched one of his animals fall to its doom (as frequently happened on the original East Rim Trail). But the title of this rock formation is a misnomer because it isn't slick at all. In fact, the sandstone that bears the name is actually quite rough to the touch, but loose grains of sand make it slippery.

The upper half of the Navajo Sandstone weathers and erodes quite readily, and many domes and slopes develop varying degrees of steepness. Such areas support very little vegetation, but they add to the variety and beauty of the scenery. Only a flight over the park, or hike in the backcountry will reveal the extent of the slickrock to be found in Zion.

EMERALD POOLS

In a short canyon opposite Zion Lodge, pools have been formed by the gouging action of two waterfalls. One of the pools is at the base of the precipitous Navajo wall and the other is below a lesser cliff. Though officially named Heaps Canyon, this area is usually referred to as Emerald Pools, a name resulting from the green tinge that algae has given the water.

A paved path, which accommodates wheelchairs and strollers,

Opposite: Kolob Arch is one of Zion's most impressive sights.
Left: View across Kolob Canyons.
Above: Backlit waterfall at Emerald Pools.
Below left: Bigtooth maple leaves turn brilliant shades of red before they fall.
Below right: Plains prickly-pear cactus.

Above: The Great White Throne.
Right: Waterfall at the Lower Pool.

leads 0.6 mile to the Lower Pool through groves of oak, maple, ash, Rocky Mountain juniper, and fir. A trail beyond the paved path goes behind the waterfall and beneath an over-hanging cliff where the seeping water deposits tufa (calcium carbonate or limestone) and gives life to the hanging gardens. The white, powdery deposit on this wall is baking soda (sodium bicarbonate). Minnows and water ouzel may be observed in the pool below.

A one-half mile, ungraded trail takes you to the Upper Pool, which is also small, but deeper than the other. The canyon wren and the diminutive winter wren can be seen darting in and out of the crevices. Scarlet lobelia blooms here in late summer.

Just on top of the cliff above the Lower Pool is yet another pool, which is hardly deep enough to wet your ankles. It is a favorite of photographers for catching reflections of the cliffs. Take care to stay well back from the edge of the cliff.

THE GREAT WHITE THRONE

Looming 2,000 feet above the river, the Great White Throne is probably the best, and most accessible display of the full depth of Navajo Sandstone anywhere.

Only the top half of the throne is white, but even that may not appear so without the late afternoon sunlight. Moss, lichens, and mineral stains alter or conceal much of the natural color of the rock.

The back of this peak was first scaled in 1929 by Bill Evans, a Californian who did a solo climb to the summit. He fell on the way down but was rescued by rangers and recovered completely.

Paintings of the Great White Throne have hung in railroad depots across the nation, and a stamp bearing a picture of it was issued in 1934.

Z I O N

Pine Creek Bridge

The arch bridge that spans Pine Creek was completed in 1930 as part of the Zion-Mt. Carmel Highway. This impressive, man-made structure was the brainchild of Harry Langley, an engineer and landscape architect for the National Park Service.

Langley wanted the bridge to be made of local stone that incorporated every color found in the park. He began his design by cutting a sheet-metal template for each stone in the face of the bridge. Since this plan was too laborious and expensive, he built a miniature of the bridge out of green laundry soap.

The Reynolds-Ely Company, the primary contractor on the Mt.

Carmel section of the road, was also the contractor for this project. Lou Whitney, a bridge builder from Springville, Utah, was the project foreman. More than 50 men worked on quarrying, transporting, dressing, and laying the rock, most of which was obtained from huge boulders that had fallen to the base of the talus slopes from Moenave and lower Navajo Formations. Oak Creek Canyon was the primary source of rock.

Park visitors can decide for themselves whether or not the architect was successful in incorporating all of Zion's colors into this unique bridge.

Above: A misty curtain of water at Weeping Rock.
Top right: Maples near the Temple of Sinawava.
Far right: Icicles on the weeping wall.

TEMPLE OF SINAWAVA

Seven miles from the South Entrance, the scenic drive terminates in a giant rotunda with the sky as its dome. A remnant of the Navajo Sandstone wall projecting into the canyon is now eroded into a low fin. Though not actually a box canyon (one without outlets), the fin helps give the illusion of one. This serrated formation ends in a slender column about 150 feet high. It has been named "The Pulpit" and the other part of the fin is called "The Altar." The "Temple," of course, is the area surrounded by two-thousand-foot-high perpendicular cliffs. From a narrow hanging valley (a tributary valley ending high above the main valley floor) on the west wall, one of Zion Canyon's most spectacular waterfalls drops nearly 1,000 feet, provided it is raining or snow is melting on the West Rim.

The Temple of Sinawava is a good place to watch the busy water ouzel along the river, and listen for the songs of other birds such as the black-headed grosbeak, warbling vireo, or canyon wren.

This is the head of the Gateway to the Narrows Trail and the termination of the top-to-bottom Narrows hike. An interpretive display, a modern restroom, and a drinking fountain are provided for the convenience of visitors.

Looking down the canyon, one can easily recognize The Great White Throne and Angels Landing. Observation Point is the white-topped formation on the left.

WEEPING ROCK

From a parking area near the base of Cable Mountain, one can walk a quarter mile up to Weeping Rock, an area that best illustrates a type of erosion known as the Zion "spring line." This process has been in progress for thousands of years and results from rainwater passing downward through porous rock until it reaches an impervious layer. Forced to move horizontally, the water eventually emerges from the canyon walls. This intersection between porous and nonporous rock is called the spring line. At Weeping Rock, a top layer of porous Navajo Sandstone meets a denser shale-and-clay layer of Kayenta Sandstone. The result is a misty curtain of water flowing out of the rock as if the rock were weeping.

The self-guided nature trail at Weeping Rock should be taken at a leisurely pace. It may be closed during December and January as ice forms giant icicles and the trail becomes hazardous as the ice melts. Areas along the trail and stream, and around the parking lot are good places to see and hear a variety of birds. The blue-gray gnatcatcher nests on the brushy hillside and the chatter of the white-throated swift can be heard from overhead. The swift and the peregrine falcon, which can also be seen in this location, are two of the fastest-flying birds in the park.

Z I O N

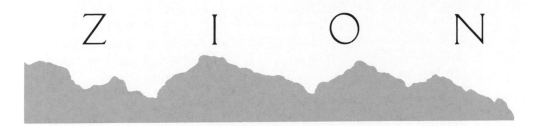

Volcanoes

Though the two most frequently visited areas of the park show little evidence of volcanic activity, Zion actually has numerous volcanic deposits. They are concentrated chiefly along the western boundary, which is also the location of minor faulting. This, of course, suggests a relationship between the faults and the volcanoes. However, the eruptions that deposited what we see today took place long after the crustal movements, and since the land acquired its present profile. Zion's volcanoes occurred within the last two million years, which is quite recent in geological terms. Some superficial changes in the landscape that resulted from the eruptions are visible along the Kolob Reservoir Road to Lava Point (see page 44).

CHECKERBOARD MESA

Checkerboard Mesa is the first named landmark a visitor sees when entering the East Entrance. This nearly cone-shaped formation is composed of the almost white upper Navajo Sandstone. Though its name is somewhat descriptive, the term "waffled" comes closer to describing the surface pattern that shows up in only a few formations in the park, and nearly always on the north face of the mountain. It is speculated that the "waffled" surface is the result of vertical cracks, which are formed by shallow fractures caused by expansion and contraction (possibly from heating and cooling) of the rock surface. These vertical cracks are superimposed on the nearly horizontal layering (the result of sedimentary processes) in the sandstone.

This fishnet pattern, called checkerboarding, is prominently displayed here on Checkerboard Mesa, on the Beehive, above the Streaked Wall, and in a few places on the West Rim Trail.

THE KOLOB RESERVOIR ROAD TO LAVA POINT

The Kolob Reservoir Road is a fascinating but too often overlooked part of Zion. Beginning at the town of Virgin, 15 miles west of the South Entrance, the road runs north from there and gains 4,400 feet in elevation in 16 miles. Its ultimate destination is Lava Point, a fire lookout station located at 7,900 feet that has a view of the canyon and much of the plateau. A primitive campground is maintained nearby and several trails and off-trail hikes start there.

Originally a pioneer ranch road, it is now both a scenic drive and a thoroughfare for local ranchers. Some outstanding features to look for on the ascent are: Tabernacle Dome, the North and South Guardian Angels, Burnt Mountain, Timber Top, and Jobs Head. Jobs Head is the Navajo Sandstone cliff between Firepit Knoll and Maloney Hill. Its most significant feature is the point where the formation's color turns from white to salmon.

After leaving Virgin, the road follows North Creek for a short

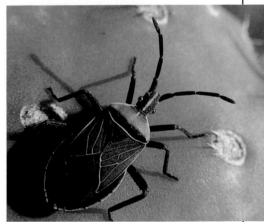

distance along the base of a mesa, which is capped by a layer of basalt that has been determined to be one million years old. The layer to your right was obviously laid down in a valley bottom, forcing the stream to find a new route. The ridge ahead, above the Sunset Canyon Ranch, illustrates that this phenomena occurred again one quarter of a million years ago. The road rises 2,300 feet in 5 1/2 miles on the lava flow that caused North Creek (on the east side) and intermittant drainages (on the west side) to incise new canyons into the softer sedimentary layers. The road levels

out for a short distance in Cave Valley, where sand from eroding Navajo Sandstone cliffs covers the underlying lava.

The road climbs again and passes Spendlove and Firepit Knolls, which are two cinder cones, more or less on the line of East Cougar Mountain Fault, and mark the last episodes of volcanic activity in Zion. Firepit Knoll, north of the road, is red instead of the black one would expect a volcanic crater to be. To the south, Lee Valley has developed along the East Cougar Mountain Fault, and is partially filled with lava. Hop Valley, not visible from the road, has

Top left: Checkerboard Mesa.
Top right: Ponderosa pine seedling.
Above: Beetle commonly found on prickly-pear cacti.
Far left: View of West Temple from Kolob Reservoir Road.

Z I O N

Who Named What

It has long been the policy of the U.S. Geological Survey to accept the first, or oldest, place-name as official. Zion Canyon was named by its first Mormon settler, a farmer named Isaac Behunin. One evening while sitting on his front porch in the lingering twilight, he gazed across the vast expanse of the canyon. He was so moved by its grandeur that it inspired him to remember a passage in the Bible (Isaiah 2:2), which mentions a place called Zion, found "in the top of the mountains," where "the Lord's house shall be established." Isaac felt that he had discovered such a place, and from that moment on, he called it Zion.

Many of the names for individual features within the park were given by park officials, and the logic behind most choices is obvious. One red peak with an arch became Red Arch Mountain, and another became Lady Mountain when someone saw in it the likeness of a woman.

Johnson Mountain was named for the canyon's discoverer, Nephi Johnson. A visiting Methodist minister, Frederick Fisher, and two of his friends, were responsible for labeling the Three Patriarchs, the Great White Throne, and Angels Landing. Other features were tagged by topographers and scientists, or named after local residents.

Despite discouragement from park officials, cattle are often seen grazing in open areas in Hop Valley and Kolob Canyons.

developed along the East Cougar Mountain Fault, draining to the north.

A trail starts near Spendlove Knoll and leads across private land, and down Hop Valley to Kolob Arch, a distance of seven miles. This is one of several approaches to the arch, making it advisable to get information at either visitor center before venturing into this area.

The story of Hop Valley is the same as that of upper Zion Canyon in that it has a flat sandy bottom, which was caused by a landslide. A small meandering stream makes for a pleasant segment of trail where grazing cattle may be encountered, since part of the valley is privately owned. Visitors to the backcountry are advised that all water must be treated before use as it is subject to contamination.

After crossing the head of Lee Valley, the road ascends Maloney Hill where still another, and much older (1.4 million years) lava flow drapes over a Navajo Sandstone cliff. Immediately to the west is Jobs Head, the point where the Navajo Sandstone changes from white to red. The road ascends further, mostly on a lava base and among protruding buttes of Navajo and Temple Cap Sandstone, to finally top out into Carmel shales. Home Valley Knoll, another basaltic cone, appears to the right of the road near the turnoff to Lava Point. It is thought to be the source of the thick layer of basalt that forms Lava Point.

The last 3 1/2 miles of the road to Lava Point are not paved. Though there are other roads by which one may descend the mountain, they are steep and dusty. Visitors should obtain information at one of the visitor centers regarding weather and road conditions.

From Lava Point, one has a panoramic view of Zion Canyon from the top side, and a view of the gray and pink layers of the Cenozoic Era and the Cretaceous Period to the east and north. On a clear day Mt. Trumbull, near the North Rim of the Grand Canyon, is also visible.

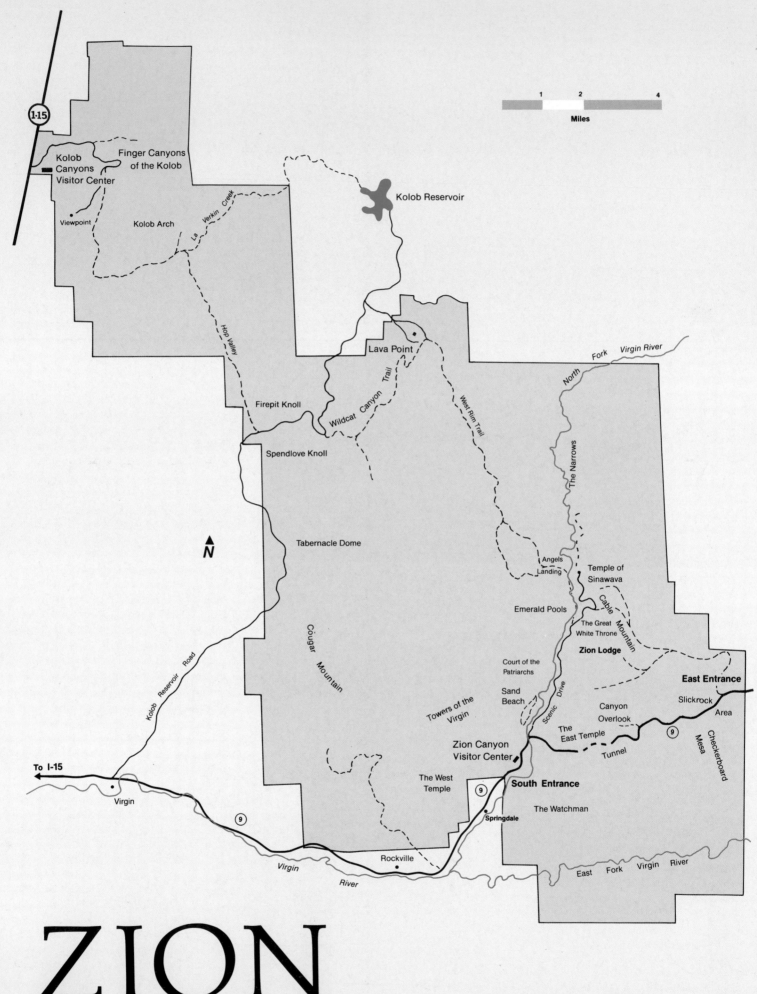

ZION
NATIONAL • PARK